"Live your life by the universal laws that govern health, happiness and abundance."

The 7 Spiritual Laws of Prosperity

And How to Manifest Them in Your Life

By Randy Gage

Gage, Randy.
   The 7 spiritual laws of prosperity : and how to
manifest them in your life / by Randy Gage. — 1st ed.
p. cm.
"Live your life by the universal laws that govern
 health, happiness and abundance."
LCCN 2003102891
ISBN 0971557853

   1. Success—Psychological aspects. 2. Conduct of life.
I. Title.

BF637.S8B34 2003   158.1
                              QBI33-1269

"The 7 Spiritual Laws of Prosperity" is part of a five-book series on Prosperity by Randy Gage.

101 Keys to Your Prosperity

Accept Your Abundance! Why You are supposed to be Wealthy

37 Secrets About Prosperity

The 7 Spiritual Laws of Prosperity and How to Manifest Them in Your Life

Prosperity Mind: How to Harness the Power of Thought

Published by:
Prime Concepts Publishing
A Division of Prime Concepts Group, Inc.
1807 S. Eisenhower Street
Wichita, Kansas 67209-2810 USA

Order Information:
To order more copies of this book, or to receive a complete catalog of other products by Randy Gage, contact:

Prime Concepts Group, Inc.
1-800-946-7804 or (316) 942-1111
or purchase online at:
www.RandyGage.com
www.Prosperity-Insights.com

Dedication

To Juanito.

Acknowledgements:

I would like to express special thanks to Ford, Alicia and Cyndy at Prime Concepts Group for turning this project around so fast, and so well. It's an honor working with you guys.

Table of Contents

Forward
By Lisa Jimenez, M.Ed.

I'm driving up to Disney World with my three kids. We were in our brand new truck. We have two laptop computers (chock full of games), a movie playing on our portable DVD player, two CD players, and a Game Boy. My son Beau says he is bored and doesn't know what to do with the time . . .

So, it's very clear that "stuff" is NOT prosperity. In fact, WANTING more and not finding satisfaction in what you have is the opposite of prosperity—this is actually poverty—poverty of the mind and spirit.

I'd even go so far to say that Health, Wealth, and Happiness are not prosperity! These things are contingent on circumstance. And circumstance is not in our control. Prosperity is not about circumstance.

To me, prosperity is a state of mind. It is innate JOY. This deep JOY is not contingent of my circumstance. If my Armani suit gets dirty, my brand new Lexus rusts, I get sick, I lose money, or a loved one dies; my happiness might flee, but my innate JOY still exists.

This innate JOY is Prosperity.

Prosperity is the quiet, confident assurance of who you are and whose you are. And that is enough. The ironic thing is, this prosperity is exactly what I need to manifest health, wealth, and happiness.

I look at the Apostle Paul, whose experiences varied from poverty, abundant wealth, and everything in between, and I see someone who was content in any and every situation. How was he able to do this? Where did he find his source of contentment?

He knew who he was and whose he was.

This is what Apostle Paul says in the letter he wrote to the Philippians:

"True prosperity is peace in your circumstances. I know what it is to be in need, and I know what it is to have plenty. I have learned the secret of being content in any and every situation, whether well fed or hungry, whether living in plenty or in want. I can do everything through Him who gives me strength. I rely on His promises." (Phil. 4:12)

Paul also said, "Focus on what you are called to do, not what you feel you should have. Detach self from the nonessentials so that you can concentrate on the eternal."

The answer to experiencing prosperity and finding true contentment lies in:

- Your perspective;
- Your priorities; and,
- Your source of power.

Randy Gage has insights into all these areas. A modern-day scholar, he has spent 15 years studying the science of prosperity, and the connection between what we think, and what we manifest. In this book he offers some thought-provoking insights into the subject. Whether you agree with him or dispute what he says, he bears listening to, because he is a man who knows who he is, and whose he is.

Introduction:
Does God Really Exist?

I had a fascinating dinner last week. It was with a large group that wound down by the end to a fundamentalist Christian, a Jew, an agnostic, an atheist, a new thought Christian, and me. So naturally I couldn't resist bringing up the delicious issue of religion and whether God exists.

It should come as no surprise to you, but even though we talked 'til way past the restaurant's closing time, we didn't definitively settle the issue. But what a captivating and enthralling conversation that ensued! Exactly the kind of discourse I relish.

Here was the fascinating thing to me. I am a Christian. I believe in Jesus Christ as both a historical figure and a spiritual one. But as the discussion bounced back and forth—primarily between the fundamentalist Christian versus the agnostic and atheist—I kept nodding in agreement to most everything the two non-believers had to say.

Why?

Because they had come to their beliefs after a great deal of introspection, critical analysis and conscious thought. While my fundamentalist friend just kept parroting the inane clichés she learned at 8 years old in her catholic school, and claiming they were "proof" because the Bible says so.

Of course, from a rational, logical point of view, the idea of God existing is impossible to substantiate.

Now notice that I said from a rational and logical basis. That does not mean that God does not exist. (Although a strong argument can be made that He/She does not.) What it does mean is that the proof of God existing cannot be determined from a rational or logical point of view.

Now fundamentalists, before you write me - please make sure you really understand the meaning of those two words, rational and logical. Because Psalms 14:1 says, "The fool says in his heart, 'There is no God'" - does not qualify as consistent with reason and intellect. Nor do the other 25 scripture verses you want to quote me to "prove" that God exists.

Now I could write quite a book here refuting the different ways theists would try to prove that God exists. Mostly, they can all be categorized in three schools of thought.

First would come natural theology—we can't explain everything in the universe and how it got here, therefore there must be a supernatural being or force behind it all.

Next would be the cosmological arguments; every existing thing has a cause, and every existing cause must be caused by a prior cause. So either we have an endless chain of prior causes, or we had one first cause, namely, "In the beginning, God created the heavens and the earth."

Third, would be the design arguments. These arguments are centered on the case that everything in nature is by design, so we must conclude that there was a master designer, something or someone omnipotent and omniscient (God).

Now I said I could write a book refuting all three of these arguments on a rational, logical basis—and demonstrate that they cannot be proven. But that is NOT my goal here, to disprove either the existence of God, or whether it can be proven. I am saying that the usual things theists trot out to "prove" the existence of God do nothing of the sort.

I believe that when you question your beliefs—if the beliefs are true and serve you—they will withstand any scrutiny you give them.

The reason I kept nodding in agreement to many of the things my agnostic and atheist friends at dinner were saying, is because they made such a convincing case for their beliefs, and it was obvious that they came by their beliefs after a great deal of critical thought. It should be noted that the atheist is a former minister, who graduated from Oral Roberts University. He came to his beliefs after many years of soul searching, research, and study.

So while I don't agree with his conclusions, he has my utmost respect, because he is not just parroting something his church, temple or synagogue taught him when he was six years old. He's a brilliant guy, and came to his decision after conscious introspection. In fact, you will find quite a large number of intellectual heavyweights are agnostic or atheist.

I came to the issue from the other end of the spectrum. I was an atheist for the first 26 or 27 years of my life. After some serious introspection, and what I believe is a spiritual revelation (and my atheist friends would probably view as mystical hallucination)—I came to believe in God. And shortly thereafter, became a Christian.

My problem with my fundamentalist Christian friend (which is the same problem I have with fundamentalists of all faiths), is not just the arrogance and intolerance of her beliefs, but the fact that she is just repeating the script programmed into her by the nuns in the California Catholic school she was reared in.

She didn't come to her beliefs by conscious thought, and is afraid to question them. Had she been born and raised in Iran, Pakistan, or some other country, she would likely be covering her face in public, wearing a burqa and preaching how the infidel Christians are actually Satan in disguise.

Did you come to your religious beliefs (or the lack of them) by conscious thought, or simply accept programming from your family and/or religious institution?

I do believe in God. I don't harbor the delusion that his existence can be proven with rational evidence. Or at least not at our current level of scientific understanding. However, I do believe that . . .

Spiritual things must be discerned spiritually.

Now having said that, I believe that prosperity is governed by spiritual laws. And these spiritual laws operate in very rational, logical ways, just as the law of gravity does.

So, the book you are about to read will journey into both worlds; spirituality and rationality. And if I have done my job right, it will cause you to question some beliefs that you hold to be true. So I hope you do question what you read intensely. But more importantly, I hope you apply it. Because the real proof is in the manifestation.

I can tell you that the discovery and implementation of these laws allowed me to turn my life around from abject poverty to abundant riches. I wrote this book so you can do the same!

Randy Gage
Hollywood, Florida
March 2003

Chapter One
Prosperity Consciousness

On Concorde, Somewhere over the Atlantic . . .

I'm writing this chapter hurtling 58,000 feet above the earth at slightly faster the Mach II. (For those of you keeping score at home, that's 1,340 mph.)

I'm aboard British Airways flight 001, on the flagship of their fleet, flying back to the States from a prosperity seminar I conducted in London over the weekend.

It's funny. When I race my Viper (at speeds around 150 mph), I wear a fire-resistant driver's suit, gloves and shoes, a Bell crash helmet, and a 5-point safety harness. My fellow passengers are sipping Dom Perignon with their Beluga caviar. No one is wearing fire suits or crash helmets, as they casually stroll to the lavatories in between meal courses. What better demonstration of the prosperity possible from human progress!

I got a chance to experience and talk about prosperity quite a bit over the weekend. It started with my arrival at the airport. I got there about two hours early, figuring the security hassles at JFK for an international flight would be arduous. I discovered that as a Concorde passenger, you have a private check in, and are whisked to a private security line. From there, you enter "The Concorde Room," where you are pampered with private waiters to serve you champagne, breakfast and other snacks. When you land, instead of waiting behind the 500 people lined up for customs, you hop over to a special line that takes you five minutes.

Just viewing the plane from the terminal is an experience. It looks like a majestic bird of prey, and sitting dead motionless, it still looks like it's racing along at trans sonic speed. Grown men are reduced to kids, gawking and murmuring; beseeching strangers to photograph them with it. Flight time over to London on Friday was 3 hours and 14 minutes. Heading back now, we're fighting a headwind, so it will take us a terminally long 3 hours and 22 minutes!

Stop two of my prosperity weekend was a visit to see John Lobb, Bootmaker, in central London. The Lobb family has been making handcrafted footwear for a couple of generations, for everyone from The Prince of Wales to Andrew Carnegie, from The Duke of Edinburgh to Frank Sinatra.

It's kind of funny, but I see shoes as a yardstick for my prosperity consciousness.

Growing up always with two pairs of shoes ("gym" shoes and "dress" shoes), I remember being incredulous to hear that there were people who actually spent $200 on a pair of shoes. I thought that was positively obscene.

As I began to make some money and discover the finer things in life, I came to learn about Bally loafers. They are made of the softest leather, and mold to your feet like warm butter. When I bought my first pair, I felt like I had ascended the pinnacle of wealth and opulence, because I now spent more on a pair of shoes ($300) than I used to spend on a car. I didn't think you could get any richer!

As my journey to the good life continued, I discovered the joy of elegant designer shoes from Prada and others, which meant doubling the amount I paid for footwear.

From there, I graduated to Testoni shoes, the perfect compliment to a stylish business suit. Now I was above the $1,000 a pair range, which stretched the limits of even my prosperity consciousness.

But when you buy things on the high end of the spectrum, you discover something quite interesting...

There really is a difference. Complete strangers stop you and compliment you on your shoes. You can wear them all day and they still feel great. And a quality pair of shoes will last you a lifetime.

And then you walk in to Lobb's of London . . .

You pick out the style you like, choose the exact leather, color, and select the type of heel. Then both your feet are measured by the fitter at four spots. He then traces your feet, noting the precise statistics and every individual feature.

From here it goes to the last-maker, whose brilliance is his ability to use this information to carve a solid maple model of your feet.

Next in the process is the clicker. He is the leather expert whose vast experience in hides and skins allows him to choose and cut the eight pieces of leather that will be used to craft the upper part of your shoe.

These pieces will go to the closer, who will cut and stitch the leather around the last of your foot.

Then it goes to the maker who takes this carefully assembled upper, and adds the sole of the best English tanned, oak-bark leather, and the layered riveted heel.

Lobb maintains that their makers are so precise that they can tell you the exact number of stitches needed to give maximum strength to the union of soul and upper on any particular shoe.

After the maker completes the sole, he adds the details like eyelets and inner soles, and then sends them to the polisher.

Who shines their shoes to their pristine glory. Another pair of shoes from Lobb the Bootmaker has been born! And so has another increase in my prosperity consciousness. I won't bludgeon you with the cost, but I will tell you this. Just the shoetrees that come with them cost over $600!

So is it worth it? Is it obscene to be spending that kind of money on a pair of shoes? How could anyone spend that on shoes, when there are children starving in Africa . . . diseases needing funding for a cure . . . mistreated animals that need to be rescued . . . etc./etc.?

Well those are some intriguing questions. Before we answer them, let's head back the other direction, to a hotel in California . . .

It was established in 1875. It was the belle of the San Francisco social scene for almost a century. Then, alas, the Palace Hotel faded from glory, a ghost of her once illustrious past.

Now after many millions of dollars and a complete renovation, the Palace is once again, The Palace. If the freshly decorated splendor doesn't convince you, then the $1.50 surcharge for local phone calls will.

Which raises an interesting prosperity issue . . .

I recently conducted a Mastermind Retreat for the top level of my coaching program in Las Vegas. We selected the Aladdin Hotel because some of the Mastermind Council members had been grumbling about the high hotel rates on some of our exotic trips. So I went along with the idea of having one luxury trip a year, and one that was more affordable.

Two minutes inside the Aladdin made me realize what a mistake that was. (Although I had my suspicions when the taxi driver told me that everyone he picked up there complained about it, and that there was no water pressure or hot water on the top floors.)

Now it's hard to believe that you can spend over a billion dollars building a place and not have it be nice. But if you need proof, the Aladdin's the place.

The world's first billion-dollar-dump. But back to our prosperity dilemma . . .

One of my Council members complained that the hotel was charging him 25 cents a page to make some copies. I told him to get over it and concentrate on more prosperous things.

Easy for me to say—until I found out they were charging me $25 a day to work out in the fitness center. In a fitness center that you would expect to find in a Holiday Inn.

No, I take that back. I apologize Holiday Inn.

The Aladdin also levies a $5 surcharge to receive an overnight letter. And one dollar a page to receive a fax. And for Michael Bolton's sake, I hope he never has to get a haircut there. Mine cost me $59.

I look at his hair, and then at mine—or more specifically the absence of it—and I can only extrapolate that Michael's haircut would cost him $15,724.

So the question raised—and it's a good one—is where does prudently managing your money end, and living prosperous begin?

It's a fascinating issue . . .

Is it over the top to pay $400 a night for a hotel room, when there are others available for $89? What about $800 a night? And what about a $4,000 a night suite?

What would you think about paying $10,000 for a purse? There were several available in the Bellagio shops in Vegas. Along with a gorgeous $10,000 ostrich coat.

Here at the Palace, I'm having a fresh fruit cup and granola for breakfast. This little repast will set me back about twenty-five bucks. Not even a block down the street, there's a McDonalds where I could fill up for $2.

I think I'll stay here.

First, I'm eating a breakfast that will prolong my life, not shorten it. The orange juice is freshly squeezed, and I have a beautiful blue glass vase with two fresh-cut roses on my table. Classical music is playing over the sound system, and everyone is dressed elegantly. Guys are pulling out chairs for ladies, and I just realized that I'm the only guy in the place without a sport coat or jacket on. At breakfast!

The dining room itself is a four-story glass atrium with towering marble columns. It would serve as an Opera house in many areas of the world! Tourists are walking by just to gawk at the ceiling. There is a large round table in the center with a floral arrangement. This arrangement probably set the hotel back more money than ninety percent of the people in the world pay a month for rent. There are enough ferns and other greenery in here to stock an aviary.

Can you really compare that with sitting on a plastic bench, staring at Ronald McDonald memorabilia, choking down food with enough cholesterol to drop a stallion?

If you think a car is just transportation from point A to point B, you've never ridden in a Rolls Royce, or drove a Ferrari. If you think shoes shouldn't cost more than $100, you've never slipped your feet into Bally or Santoni loafers. Or never "finished off" the perfect outfit with just the right pair of gator, croc, or ostrich shoes.

Yes the price difference between a first class seat and one in economy is a great deal. But you might find it is worth it if you are more than 5'6" tall, weigh more than 120 pounds, or want to open a laptop computer. If you want to work (or sleep) on the trip; if you want to be treated with respect and not like cattle; and if you want to arrive relaxed—it could certainly be worth the extra money.

Here's my take on all this . . .

Paying 25 cents a copy isn't justified by any extra value. The quality is the same as the copies you get for ten cents. But the insignificant amount of money we're taking about doesn't justify my spending any time worrying about it.

It's also hard to justify paying $25 to work out in a fitness room that would be free any place else, or a dollar a page to receive a fax. This is just petty extortion. But that doesn't mean I'm looking for bargains . . .

I'm happy to pay $25 for breakfast at the Palace, $5,000 for a bespoke suit, and six figures for the right sports car.

Why?

Because those things offer a dramatic step up in quality from their lower priced alternatives. When it comes to prosperity, I have a simple belief:

Life is too short to fly coach!

Is it because I think I'm "too good" to fly in economy?

Well now that you mention it, yes I do! If my head falls back over the seat, because it was designed 40 years ago, when the average person was a foot shorter . . . if the guy next to me is spilling over the armrest into my seat . . . if the seat in front of me is pressing against my knees . . . if I cannot even read the screen on my laptop, because I can't open it all the way . . . then yes I am too good to ride back there. And you are too!

I don't believe it serves God, serves you, or serves anyone for you to live your life in the coach section. I think it's a crime for you to be unhappy, unhealthy, or struggling for existence. **In fact, I think it is a deviation of your Divine nature for you to settle for lack or limitation in any area of your life.**

Now we know from Lisa's Forward that "stuff" won't make us happy, and isn't the yardstick to measure prosperity. Material possessions can make your life more comfortable, without a doubt. And I hope you have a lot of them. And I know that your relationship with a force greater than you, is the true source of your prosperity.

A very prosperous man once remarked, "Strive first for the kingdom of God and his righteousness, and all these things will be given to you as well." I put God first in my life, and recognize that Divine Spirit is the source for all the many blessings I have in my life, and give thanks that this is true.

I would love to write a prosperity book that had nothing about God in it, because it might reach out to more people. But I couldn't do that, because as I told you in the introduction, the beliefs I have in this area wouldn't allow me to.

Don't get me wrong. I'm not here to convert you, or challenge your particular faith.   But I am sharing my thoughts, experiences and insights on prosperity, as I know them to be true. And I think being spiritually grounded is an integral part of that.

And I also think that "stuff" comes into play as well. I believe prosperity is a composite of many things. Spiritual sustenance. Abundant health. Meaningful relationships. Fulfilling work. Intellectual growth. And material possessions.

You will never hear me say something like, "Prosperity is more than 'just' money." Because doing so diminishes money. I believe having money is the fastest way to demonstrate who you are, and what you are about. I do believe that money is God in action.   Desire is what drives your soul to evolve.

There is no doubt that prosperity is appreciating a spring shower, the waves crashing on the shore, and the wings of a butterfly. Prosperity is having a strong connection with your creator, having people who bring joy to your life, and holding a newborn baby. And prosperity is also having beautiful clothes, living in your dream home (or homes), and having a car (or a garage full of cars) that makes your heart race!

I have simple pleasures in my life. When I'm playing softball and I swing the bat just right, and meet the ball just right, and it sails over the fence for a home run, that's a spiritual experience for me. When I wake up and see the sun rising over the ocean, that's a spiritual experience as well. Supporting my church is meaningful to me, and brings a spiritual reward for me as well.

But make no mistake. Those spiritual experiences are enhanced because of the money I have!

I have been successful, and can now schedule my work on my terms, and play in four softball leagues. Everyone can appreciate a sunrise. But I think it is even more spiritual for me, because I can do that in my own condo, every single day, not once a year, staying at a hotel. I can support my church, because I am no longer struggling to pay my bills. I am able to help others, because I have helped myself first.

The number of people teaching prosperity seminars that have no money amazes me. They say things like, "I may not have manifested a lot of money, but I have my health, and I feel prosperous no matter where I am."

Great. I'm glad they are happy. But I believe if you have to worry about paying the rent, wonder if your car will break down, or fear that you won't have enough to send your kid to a good college—you are not experiencing true prosperity.

I believe that you are not given desires without also being given the resources to manifest them. And I believe that manifesting them is what brings you further down your path of spiritual development. I believe in what Reverend Eric Butterworth calls "Divine Dissatisfaction."

I'm not satisfied flying in the sardine section. Or with cheap shoes. Or greasy food. And I believe that comes from God. So the real issue we are dealing with here is the question of, "How much is enough?"

Now that is an interesting question. Because I happen to think this is probably one of the worst lack expressions ever uttered. Just the tone and predisposition of the question implies negativity.

You hear it when you read about a professional athlete getting a big contract, someone winning a large amount in the lottery, or a very wealthy person earning more money.

"I guess he couldn't get by on ten million a year. He left to play for another team at $12 million."

"She won $57 million. I don't need that much. I'd be happy with one million."

"He's already worth $4 billion and he's building another hotel. Just how much is enough anyway?"

Notice how these statements are derogatory by their very nature. Each one implies that the person being talked about is unreasonable or greedy. The implication is that the "extra" money that they are taking is coming from your pocket.

Example: *"That's why ticket prices are so high. These guys get paid too much."*

Sounds good, looks good, looks good on paper. Just not true. The reason athletes get paid so much is because they draw fans to their sport. People go to the stadiums, and they watch on TV. If they didn't, the team would lose money and go out of business. In fact, it's a good investment for teams to have a few superstars that draw more fans. That's what drives the sport.

Teams only pay for players because they make them more money. (The exception here is Major League Baseball. Because they have an antitrust exemption. The sport isn't regulated by the free market economy, but the ignorance of the owners and current commissioner.)

If you let the free market prevail, it will always equalize things out. Economic factors like price and salaries will always equalize, because the free market is based on trading value for value.

And that's the real prosperity issue . . .

I mentioned that $10,000 ostrich coat I saw, and the $10,000 purse. If there are people who will pay that much for those items, they must perceive that value in them. And for us to judge their situation is wrong, because we can't know what the expenditure means to them, or what their financial situation is.

I will tell you this. I would have bought that ostrich coat in a minute, if I didn't have so many coats already, and live in a place where I can only wear them about five nights a year. It was beautiful.

In my case, I just can't justify it with myself, because I have a cashmere one, a leather one, a wool one, and about seven other ones of all kinds. Had I not just bought a new Pal Zileri bomber jacket in Paris last month, I'm sure I would have snatched up the coat. (And the fact that I'm still talking about it, lends credence to the possibility that I will fly back and get it anyway!)

Now as for that $10,000 purse, I didn't see it, and I don't know anything about it. And I have no need for a purse. But I can tell you this. Four different ladies in the Mastermind Council couldn't stop talking about it, and how beautiful it was. I could tell by the look in their eyes, that it would bring a great deal of joy to their lives. So it doesn't seem to be out of bounds to me.

Now where you are at in all this, I don't know. But I believe that you want more in your life, or you wouldn't be reading this book. And I believe you have a creator that wants you to have more, do more, and become more.

And that's why I'm writing this book for you. I believe that prosperity is all those things we talked about. And I believe that manifesting it in your life is simply a case of living your life by the spiritual laws that govern it. I've devoted a chapter to each of them. So if you are ready to receive the true prosperity that is your birthright—turn the page!

Chapter Two
The Vacuum Law of Prosperity

*The universe cannot put good into your hand, until
you let go of what you are holding in it.*

If you walk down the beach, you leave footprints in the
sand. But give the wind and the waves a few minutes,
and those tracks will be filled in. Just as vegetation will
cover a field and an agenda expands to the time
budgeted for a meeting.

Nature abhors a vacuum. And since the inherent nature of
the universe is good, a vacuum will always be filled with
good. So one of the fastest ways to manifest prosperity in
your life is to create vacuums.

One evening at the end of my prosperity class I was
teaching, one of the students walked up to me confused.
She wanted to know how all "this prosperity stuff" could be
working, since she had recently lost her job, and her
boyfriend left her.

The interesting thing was that she had been complaining
about that job for months. Her pay was miniscule, and it
seemed to offer no room for advancement. And several
times we had discussed her boyfriend, who had been both
physically and verbally abusive to her.

So actually, as I told her, she was quite likely on a very
positive path towards prosperity. Which is exactly how it
turned out for her.

As her consciousness developed, her job could no longer
hold her, and her boyfriend was no longer comfortable with

her. Ultimately she was able to get a much better job, and attract a man who appreciated her and wouldn't abuse her.

If you are holding on to something negative, there is no room for the positive to come into your life. So when people come to me for advice because they are not manifesting prosperity in all areas of their lives, the first question I ask is the one below:

What are you still holding on to—that you need to release?

This vacuum effect works in all areas of your life. When I am feeling distracted and overwhelmed with work, one look around my desk and office explains everything. Stuff piled around everywhere. My environment is cluttered and disorganized, so I feel cluttered and disorganized.

So I stop what I am doing and start sorting. I put everything in piles on the floor, according to project. Then I put each project into its own folder. Then I write a to-do list, with all the important things that need to be done for each project. Then I put the files in the cabinet or active file tray on my desk.

Even if I have 40 things on my list, I immediately relax, and approach the tasks at hand with clarity and focus. I prioritize the list, and take great joy for each item I cross off as I finish. This creates a positive energy around everything I'm doing, and before I know it, I'm done with everything I need to do.

In my case, I work better when I have inner peace and focus. So I have to release all the distractions, and create a vacuum for peace of mind. If I feel there is just too much going on in my life, I'll clean out my junk drawer or closets.

When you are surrounded by open, organized space, you feel more expansion, creative and in control. This same principle applies in attracting all areas of prosperity in your life. If you want some new shoes, give some of the ones you have away. If you want some new clothes, clean out your closet (create a vacuum) and donate some old clothes at the homeless shelter.

Want some more hugs in your life? Want more love in your life? Give some away!

Of course this same law applies to health. I had a lot of health challenges the first 30 years of my life. Just like I had a lot of financial challenges, and other personal issues. The bottom line is that I was sick, broke and stupid!

And I couldn't understand why. I came to discover that in actuality, I was manifesting all the lack in my life, because I had a victim consciousness. I was holding on to lack, because it allowed me to keep manifesting bad things . . . which allowed me to feed my noble victim scenario.

I could hang around with all my loser friends each day, and we could all commiserate about how hard it was to get ahead, how rich people had all the opportunities, how unfair life was, and other such nonsense.

I was holding on to being a victim . . . so there was no space in my mind for me to become a victor.

Once I was able to let go of my victim-hood, a whole new world of possibilities opened up for me. Health challenges that I had carried around my whole life just cleared up, at the snap of my fingers.

Don't get me wrong. The health challenges were real, and I had all kinds of medical records to prove it. But they were real because I believed they were real, and because I needed them, to hold on to being a victim. Once I no longer desired to be a victim, they miraculously were cured.

Because I no longer needed them to define who I was, my body simply released them. And regenerated healthy tissue.

Now it takes a certain amount of faith to practice this law. You have to be willing to let go of things. Once you realize that the universe is inherently good, it's easier to have faith in just outcomes. You no longer fear releasing things, because you know that they will be replaced with something of equal or even greater value.

You are surrounded by good everywhere. The only lack, is the lack in your mind. Open your mind to receive prosperity, create a vacuum to hold it, and you will attract it.

Prosperity Affirmations for Creating a Vacuum for Good:

I release all that no longer serves me, and I am open to the good that is coming to me.

I let go, and let God. I know my highest good is coming to me.

That which does not serve me, I release. I am open to the rich, bountiful good that is coming toward me.

I let go of that which is not my highest good, and I open myself up to Divine Order.

Chapter Three
The Circulation Law of Prosperity

Be willing to give away something you possess, to receive something you desire.

Think of prosperity like a brisk, flowing river. It is never standing still. It's always moving, releasing pressure, and seeking its proper level.

On the other hand, when water pools in a stationary place, it becomes cloudy and stagnant.

So this law of circulation that governs prosperity operates the same way. Misery hoarding leads to recession. When you circulate substance, you break the energy block and keep the river of prosperity flowing freely.

So for example, I never feel that I own anything, even though the title may be in my name. Even my cars and home are just in my life for a while. Then I will release them and move on. We all go through cycles. The house that you need when you are single may not be adequate when your three children arrive. Likewise when they grow up and leave home, you may wish for another, smaller place.

You safeguard and use possessions when you have them. When they no longer serve you, you release them to someone they serve. So I may sell one of my sports cars when I want to buy the new model. That serves the new owner and me. I get my new car, and he or she gets a car that is new to him or her, but at lower price than a new model would cost.

It seems every six months or a year, I upgrade to a new computer, because the newer models have more features I need, are lighter, and work faster. So I buy them, and give my old one to a friend who doesn't have one. When I am practicing the first law, and want to create a vacuum by giving away old shoes or clothes, I am invoking the second law as well.

Circulation of money brings powerful prosperity results . . .

Let's suppose that you are in a bad financial situation. You are down to your last $100, and you have $1,500 in debts. Instead of hanging on to the $100, waiting for $1,400 to appear, you put the second law, that of circulation, into practice.

You know that miserly hoarding leads to recession. So you break up the block, and start circulating what substance you have. Then you break up your $100 and send it forth into the universe with blessings.

So you tithe $10 to the source of your spiritual nourishment. Then you could send a partial payment of $20 here, $15 there, $25 some place else, etc. This breaks up the stagnant energy, and gets your money circulating. Because you are circulating money, you create an energy that attracts more substance back to you.

One other part of this. Put a blessing on your checkbook. Send out each payment by writing a blessing on your copy of the invoice and verbally repeating the blessing as you mail the checks. You will create more powerful energy to circulate more substance to you. (You'll find some possible affirmation blessings at the end of this chapter.)

Once you are out of lack, and on your way to prosperity, you can really have some fun with this law. Now you get to sow seeds! This is not your regular tithe. This is your chance to sow seeds for good.

Of course you probably start with charities that are dear to your heart. When you support these organizations, the ripple effect of your prosperity travels around the world.

For instance, I support the young artist program at several Operas. The money I sow is given to young students, so they may concentrate on the study of their craft. They use it to pay rent, buy groceries and other living expenses.

Now when they spend this money, they are also blessing their landlord, the grocer, employees and stockholders at the power company, etc. So the good is circulating again. Of course these people also possess the money a while, then they circulate it back into the universe. This cycle goes on infinitely.

Of course even more good comes from this. The artists learn their craft and become good. They perform at concerts, which bring beauty into the lives of those attending. I attend these concerts and I feel great pride and happiness for the artists I help support. It is an endless cycle of good.

Now take it one step farther . . .

I know that even with the stipend they receive, money is still tight for most of these artists. So what if I take one to lunch one day? And on the way home take him or her to my clothing shop, and buy him a concert tuxedo, or concert gown for her to perform in? It might cost $1,000, which is meaningless to me. Yet they might have to save and scrimp for a year to get that $1,000.

That $1,000 I spend won't go through the Opera fund and I won't get a tax deduction. The artist I give it to will never pay me back. I don't expect them to. It is a seed I sow.

I have given clothes to new speakers, computers to starting entrepreneurs, and sporting equipment to more youth teams than I can remember. These expenditures will never show up on my list of charitable giving, they are simply seeds that I sow.

I don't know exactly how it will come back to me. But I know it will . . .

Sometimes when you sow a seed, you get an unexpected sale, a raise or bonus. Someone you forgot about a long time ago may appear to pay money they owe you.

Or it may not show up as money at all . . .

You may get the news that your tumor is benign, your teenage daughter may start communicating with you, or you may meet your perfect soul mate.

Don't wait till you are out of debt completely or a multi-millionaire to sow seeds.   In fact, if your prosperity seems really blocked, you might want to really shake things up by sowing a seed today.

Need I tell you that you can do the same thing with love? Send love forth in circulation, and you will attract much more of it back into your life. Give away something you are no longer using, and get ready to receive your good.

Prosperity Affirmations for Circulating Prosperity:

To write on your checkbook:

You are now filled with the bounty of my Creator to supply my every need.

Money is attracted to me like a magnet.

To affirm when you are sending out payments:

I send you forth to circulate in the flow of boundless prosperity. I know that you will return to me in kind.

This is the bounty of God, and I send it forth with wisdom, faith and love.

To affirm when you are sowing a seed:

Divine love, through me, blesses and multiplies this seed of prosperity.

Chapter Four
The Imaging Law of Prosperity

You must see your prosperity in your mind first.

Prosperity, like all forms of success is created in the mind first. When you image things in your mind, you are actually programming your subconscious to manifest them on the physical plane.

One of the reasons I have affirmations after each chapter, is because these help you program your own subconscious mind. I also believe in goal cards, positive statements in your day planner, or even sticky notes with affirmations on your steering wheel, mirror, or refrigerator. When you see these reminders, you think about the thing you are trying to manifest, and that emotion anchors the thought in your subconscious mind.

The more emotions you engage, the clearer the picture is in your mind. And the clearer it is to you, the sooner you will manifest it.

In my book "Accept Your Abundance," I relate about an exercise that my friend Richard Brooke does in his seminars to help this process. He has people write a movie script of their perfect day.

So you would see into the future, the day you take your company public, you make your first million, or open that new restaurant. You want a compelling and thorough journaling of your perfect day. Remember to involve all your senses, to make the experience seem as real as possible. You want to see it, hear it, taste it, smell it, touch it, and FEEL it. It is only when you experience prosperity in your mind and heart first, that you manifest it on the physical plane.

Don't show this script to anyone, except those who support and encourage you greatly. Share it only with those you can count on as Mastermind partners toward your success.

Keep this script in someplace like your planner, briefcase, or purse, so you have it handy every day. Whenever you have a free five minutes, re-read your script. When you get stressed out during your day and feeling overwhelmed, close your door, take the phone off the hook for five minutes and study your script.

This will calm you, center you on your goal, and reinforce the positive programming in your subconscious mind. This is a very powerful tool for accepting your abundance. Here's another great one . . .

The Dream Board.

These are a lot of fun, and very powerful tools for manifesting your prosperity. This is one of the things I got out of Catherine Ponder's book, "The Dynamic Laws of Prosperity," that was very helpful to me. Here's the deal. . .

You get a big piece of poster board from the art or office supply store. You fill it with pictures, affirmations and other things you want to manifest in your life. I like to divide mine into sections, such as work, spiritual, relationships, etc.

Then in each area, you put things on the board to represent things you want to do, have, or become. So for a couple of weeks before you do this, you start collecting magazines, brochures and other materials in the hobbies and areas you are interested in.

So suppose you want to learn to play the guitar. You put a photo of one from a music magazine. But not just any guitar. You put the exact model you want to play on.

Let's say your goal is to be closer to God. You might put a religious symbol, an affirmation, or a particular scripture or quote.

Maybe you want to write a best selling book. You might cut out the New York Times bestseller list and white out the number one book and type in the title of yours. Or you could type in your name in your company's list of top producers, etc.

There are no rules for how you put things on the Board, except that the image has to mean something to you. It doesn't matter if anyone else understands it. They don't need to. But you have to know what it means every time you see it.

Be very careful what you put on your Dream Board . . .

Sherry, my vice president wanted to manifest a husband. So she found a photo of a handsome guy in a magazine, and put it on her Board.   We were sitting at lunch one day and she was discussing the new guy she was dating. She had decided that he wasn't a nice man. But he looked almost exactly like the picture she had on her Dream Board!

So she removed the picture and replaced it with a picture of a couple taken from the back, as they were strolling hand-in-hand. A short time later she met John, and they were married about three months later.

Here's another example of how powerful this technique is . . .

Back when I was still struggling, I saw a commercial for the Dodge Viper. I was almost shell shocked with how beautiful the car was, and had to own one. About a year later, I learned about Dream Boards and did my first one. I just knew I wanted a red Viper, so I put one on my Board. The magazine I had didn't have a red one, so I used a picture of a black one.

A few months later, I was negotiating a consulting contract with a company. I put a clause into the contract that when their sales reached $2 million a month, they had to buy me a new Viper. Well an interesting scenario happened.

Even before the sales quite reached there, the president of the company called me. He was so happy with the rapid progress we were making he wanted to buy me the Viper early. He was a friend of the largest Viper dealer in the world, and he had a special deal.

It seems a casino owner in Las Vegas was going through a divorce, and he had to raise some cash fast. He had a Viper with special accessory package, exotic rims, and some body modifications that had been done by the company that designed the Viper prototype for Dodge. It was the only Viper of its kind in the world.

There was only one problem . . .

It was black. So the president wanted to know if I wanted this special one, or if I wanted a red one. Now I was conflicted. I asked for some time to think.

I went out for a bike ride down Ocean Drive. About halfway down, there were two Vipers parked at the valet stand in front of a restaurant. One red, one black. Coincidence right?

I got off my bike and walked around them. I looked and looked at them from every angle, and I decided that I had to have a black one.

Since then I've had four Vipers, and the black one is still my favorite. As I look back on it, I am sure that the reason I had to have black, is because I put that black photo on my Dream Board.

In just a two-year period, I manifested everything that was on my Dream Board. So I can't encourage you strong enough to create your own. Then you place this somewhere where other people won't see it (so negative people can't ridicule it), but you see it every day. Like the other things, just walking by and seeing it out of your peripheral vision has an effect on you.

Seeing the images every day literally programs them into your subconscious mind. This creates a desire within you to take the daily action steps that bring your dreams closer to reality.

See your prosperity in your mind first. Then manifest it on the physical plane!

Prosperity Affirmations for Imaging Substance:

I see the rich bounty of God and I attract it to me now.

I see my good, and then I manifest my good.

As I envision in my mind, so I manifest on this earth.

Just as I dream it, so I will achieve it.

Chapter Five
The Creativity Law of Prosperity

Man can manifest prosperity from the ethers by the power of ideas, vision, and imagination.

Reverend Charles Fillmore taught that our creator provided for all our needs with substance, the basis for the universe. This substance is in the ethers, surrounding us everywhere on earth.   Most importantly, it responds to the mind of man, and is shaped by our thoughts.

There is no place on earth that God is not, so therefore there is abundance at every spot on earth. Substance doesn't come from "up there." You don't have to search for it, "find" it, and you don't have to "get" more of it. It is all right here, waiting for you to summon it.

You never have an idea you can't manifest—or else the Universe would be weak at its most critical point. When you transform this substance into earthbound prosperity, it's not because God heard your request and granted it. Your faith is the key to the kingdom of power within you that transcends human limitation.

So how do we convert this substance in the ethers into our prosperity? Ideas.

Everything has its origins in the mind. Ideas are the center of consciousness. Infinite mind is a repository of ideas for the resource of man. Your health, relationships, intelligence and finances are determined by the ideas you give your attention to. What you become is a result of the efforts you expend to collect these ideas.

God or the Universe doesn't withhold your good. The power to manifest your prosperity is within you. Don't look outside for the source of your supply. It comes from a power greater than you. But that power provided you with all the means you need, right inside you. You are the co-creator in your prosperity.

When I wrote the Viper clause into my consulting contract, it was an idea for manifesting my good. I have a clause in another contract right now for a Ferrari. The only limit to what you can manifest is the ideas you come up with. It all depends on how you think.

I remember conducting a prosperity class when a hand went up. Jay wanted to know how he could ever manifest more money in his life. He said he was a nurse at a hospital. It was a civil service position, he was the head nurse. And he had already reached the top of the pay scale, so a raise was impossible. As far as he could see, there was no way for him to earn more money.

I thought about it for two seconds and I asked him, "What is stopping your from opening a home healthcare agency? As a matter of fact, what about if you were to open the most exclusive one in town? An agency for the ultra-wealthy people who are sick, and want only the best, most personalized care?"

He had never thought of that. Because he was mired in lack thinking, he saw only the pay scale of his job. But wealth was simply one idea away from him. If I have learned anything about prosperity, it is this. When you have a strong vision for something, you bend the universe to your will.

On my "Prosperity" audio album I refer to this law as the Creativity Law. That's because it's all about using your creativity to pay bills, manifest wealth, and create desirable outcomes. Sometimes it's as simple as changing the way you think about something.

About ten years ago, my business was struggling. Every week, Sherry would come into my office with a big accordion file stuffed with bills. So of course it said "BILLS" on it.

After weeks of this, I finally had a revelation. Each "bill" we had was really an invoice for a blessing we had already received. For instance, when you get a bill from the power company, it's because they kept you warm in the winter, and cool in the summer, and gave you light to live by.

So we threw away that folder and got a new one that said "Blessings" on it. Then we started writing an affirmation on the envelope of every invoice that came in. (The first one listed at the end of this chapter.) It changed the whole energy of the process.

We had gotten into a "siege" mentality. Every day when the mail came we dreaded it, and had started to see the creditors as our enemy. This turned all around, and we realized again that our creditors were our partners. We talked to everyone, worked out payment plans, they worked with us, and in a few months, we were completely up to date with everyone.

There are lots of creative ways to approach a situation like this. You can write a letter to God or the Universe. Draft a note of thanks at the end of each day, giving thanks for getting closer to your dreams.

Let's say you are having difficulty with someone, maybe you're in a lawsuit with him or her, or some other disharmonious situation. Try writing a letter to their angel!

Don't write about your difficulties, however. Write about everyone involved and statements of harmony and perfect results for all concerned.

Now do I think that everyone has an angel, and they read your letter?

Probably not. But you know what? I have done this and had amazing results. We do know this . . .

At its ultimate level, everything on earth is an energy vibration. At its ultimate, ultimate level, everything is a sound vibration. Vedic sages talk about meeting in the space between thoughts. Campbell wrote about the collective unconsciousness. Is there someplace that thoughts and affirmations meet?

I don't have a clue. But as I told you, I have had amazing results with this kind of thing. It is things like this that seem silly to the uninitiated. But they actually serve to focus your energy and program your subconscious mind. Try some of these creative techniques and test the results for yourself!

God is not matter, but the Universe all around us. The Universe is substance, and this substance is available at all times to those who have learned to lay hold of its consciousness. Once you are aware of this—and you know that you have been provided with the mind to attract it—manifestation of prosperity is quite simple.

Affirmations to Invoke the Power of Creativity:

I give thanks for your immediate and complete payment.

You are immediately and completely paid through the rich avenue of Divine substance.

I see our situation resolved for the highest good of all concerned.

I tap into Divine order to manifest the means for my immediate prosperity.

Chapter Six
The Law of Giving and Receiving

You can't out give the universe.

Coming from the lack programming I had, it was very hard for me to learn this lesson. I had spent so many years as a victim, I had a difficult time believing that if I gave something away, I would receive more back. But that is really what this law is about.

As you can see, most all of these seven laws are interrelated. This one stands above them all as "the law of laws," because it is the fundamental operating principle of the Universe.

Everything in prosperity is a value-for-value equation. But the wonderful thing about all this is that what you give comes back to you in a multiple of at least ten. You can never outwit this equation. You can't out give the Universe. The more you give, the more you get back. I have been trying to out give God for more than ten years, and it can't be done. Each year I give more, and each year I am rewarded greater than the previous one.

You've also heard this law described as reaping what you sow. When you receive your blessings, it's important that you celebrate and share them. If you have a gift (whether that is playing the piano, teaching or painting) and you don't practice it, you are diminishing your Divine nature.

In order to honor your innate abilities, you must celebrate and share them. And as you do this, you attract even more blessings into your life.

All true actions are governed by this law. Nothing just "happens." There is really no such thing as luck or chance. ALL happenings are the result of some cause and can be explained in the laws of cause and effect.

We doubt this when we don't know the cause of something. But it is always there. What we know as "miracles" are things controlled by causes we don't yet understand.

Every circumstance in your life right now is the result of causes that you created. So if you want to change your circumstances, change what you are giving out. Remember that for every ten percent of effort you expend, you get back 100 percent.

Think back to our earlier lesson on sowing seeds. This law is the one that determines the results that you manifest from doing that.

Now just as you can attract and multiply your good, unfortunately, it can work the other way as well. Let's suppose that you gossip about a co-worker. You are creating a negative karma debt that must be paid. And the price is also times ten.

This applies any time you enrich yourself at the expense of another, no matter how unintentional. Let me give you an idea of what I mean . . .

My favorite show used to be "COPS." Then for some reason, I got away from it, and didn't see it for a few years. Then I was in a hotel the night before a seminar, and I started surfing channels looking for "Baseball Tonight." As I was doing this, I stumbled across COPS. I thought, "Great, I haven't seen this show in a long time. I love it."

That lasted about five minutes, and I had to turn the show off. The officers got a domestic disturbance call. They arrived to find a drunken, drug addicted woman, who had been beaten up by her boyfriend or husband. When the officers went after the man, the woman recanted her story, and started defending him. (As abuse victims often do.) As I was watching all this, my skin was crawling.

I realized that this whole show was really just voyeurism into the tragedies of some very unfortunate people. Now I knew why I had grown away from it. As my prosperity consciousness developed, the shows I watched, the books I read, and the movies I went to changed. Intuitively I had moved away from COPS and other shows like it.

This is really an issue for you today . . .

The networks have figured out that "reality" shows are cheap to produce, and that ignorant people will do anything to get on TV. Of course there still are the daytime talk shows, which are just as disgusting.   These shows play off of the ignorance of the people appearing on them for your entertainment. This is just another form of gossip, and will diminish your prosperity should you choose to watch these kinds of shows.

Give only good and you will get back only good. This law works that way, all the time, with no exceptions. Ain't it great?

Giving Affirmations:

*I send forth this substance knowing that it will
bless the giver and the receiver.*

*Divine love, through me, blesses and multiples, all
that I am, all that I have, all that I give,
and all that I receive.*

*I honor all those I come in contact with today,
and see the Divinity in all.*

*I know the Universe is good, and I send forth
my own good to be multiplied.*

Chapter Seven
The Law of Tithing

The universe will always get its tithe.

Imagine if I give you this offer. I will have American Express issue a second card for my account, with your name on it. You can use this card anywhere it is accepted, and you can buy anything you like. There is no spending limit.

If you want to buy a new wardrobe you can. If you pick out two Ferraris and a Bentley, that's cool. Even buy a new house if you can find a developer who accepts credit cards. You can buy absolutely anything you want!

This is the only condition . . .

When the bill comes every month, you have to pay ten percent of it. So buy whatever you want, just know that you pay ten cents on the dollar. Now is that a great deal or what?

Wouldn't you jump at an opportunity like that?

You already have one! It's called the Universe Express card.

Tithing is a spiritual law dating back thousands of years. It is simply the action of giving back to the source of your spiritual sustenance. Usually your church, temple, mosque or synagogue. The word tithe comes from Latin and means tenth. Tithing is giving back ten percent to God.

This is different from randomly sowing seeds, and different from the money you give to charity. The principle behind tithing is that you give it back to the source where you receive your spiritual sustenance.   It is also one of the laws that the most people seem to have difficulty accepting.

Think of it another way. Instead of thinking you are giving ten percent to God of what is yours—have you ever considered that God is giving you 90 percent of what is His?

Now the question always comes up, "Is that ten percent of the net or the gross?'

The gross. Yes the one before taxes.

Of course I never tithed for the first 30 years of my life. Think about how much money I saved!

What a joke. I used to make $11,000 a year, $15,000, $20,000. Now I tithe more than that! (And of course I had been paying my tithe anyway, just doing it involuntarily at the transmission shop, the hospital and repair shop.)

Now I will be the first to admit that tithing is a leap of faith. Let me give you an idea of how it came about . . .

My business had been seized by the tax authorities for non-payment of taxes. That put me $55,000 in debt, and I had no job, no car, and no bank account. I had been borrowing money to live on from friends for weeks, and that was drying up.

I got macaroni and cheese, at four boxes for a dollar if I bought the supermarket brand. That's all I had eaten for weeks. I was down to my last $20 when someone recommended that I buy the Ponder book I told you about earlier. I think it was $12. So if I bought it I would be down to eight. So the decision was get 80 boxes of macaroni and live for another 23 days, or get the book and eat for another eight days.

I decided that if I was going to die of starvation, it was better to get it over quickly. So I took a chance on the book.

In the book, she said I had to tithe, if I wanted to manifest prosperity in my life. I was so desperate to believe her that I did.   So out of my last eight, I put one of them in the basket at church. (And I forlornly watched it go all the way down the aisle!)

The next day I received a check from the electric company for $75. The letter with it said that they had been reviewing their records and because I was such a good customer that paid on time, they no longer needed a deposit from me.

Now that was amazing! Because I had to be one of the worst deadbeat customers they ever had. I paid my bill late every month, and they had actually turned off my lights for nonpayment three times.

I was (and am) convinced that I got that refund because I tithed at church that Sunday. Now if you analyzed it you would figure out that if I got the check on Monday, it must have been mailed the previous Friday, two days before I gave that dollar in church. You're right.

So how do I explain it?   *I can't.*

All I know is I was afraid NOT to tithe after that check came, so I tithed on that check. And one guy who had owed me $200 for two years and had disappeared— reappeared and paid me. So I tithed on that.

And I've been tithing ten percent of every dollar I have ever made since then. And every single year I earn more than the year before. Only now I don't do it out of fear. I tithe joyfully, lovingly, and gratefully.

You never know how your tithe will come back to you. Money is a pretty common way. But it could also come in the form of a reconciliation with someone you're estranged from, a gift, a new relationship, a healing, or a promotion. There are many ways your good can come back to you.

Here's what I also believe. The universe will always get its tithe. You can do it voluntarily, or by force. But you will always pay.

All those years I never tithed, I was always having my car break down, losing paychecks, having medical bills, and every other conceivable thing that kept me broke.

Remember, prosperity is about circulation. You have to keep your substance circulating, or it gets stagnant. When you tithe by choice, you invoke many of the other laws, including the law of giving and receiving, creating ripples of giving and abundance that eventually find their way back to you.

Tithing Affirmations:

Divine love, through me, blesses and multiplies, all that I am, all that I have, all that I give, and all that I receive.

I give thanks for the good that has come and is still coming to me.

I celebrate the source of my abundance and give thanks for its continued manifestation.

Thank you God!

Chapter Eight
The Law of Forgiveness

If you cannot forgive, you cannot accept abundance.

I woke up in the recovery room, with the doctor hovering over my bed. He told me that they had a hard time finding the bullet in my body, but they got it out. Then he casually mentioned that as long as they were in there, they took out my appendix.

"What! Why would you do that? I asked. "The gunshot wound is on the other side."

"Oh it's just standard procedure," he replied. "Whenever we open anyone up for anything, we take it out as a precaution. That way you won't have problems later. You don't need it anyway."

I was incredulous. I simply couldn't imagine the arrogance and audacity of someone who thought they knew better than God what organs I needed in my body, and would cut something out of my body, without even asking me.

I left the hospital a few days later with a great deal of resentment. To make matters worse, the surgery didn't work out very well. The sutures came undone, and I looked down to see blood all over my shirt one day. That necessitated another trip to the hospital.

A week after that, it became infected, requiring another hospital visit. And the pain was unbearable. It didn't matter if I was lying down, sitting or standing. I couldn't find a position that relieved the agony I was in.

As the months wore on, I didn't seem to be getting better, but actually worse. I woke up four or five times a night in a cold sweat. I had no energy, and my body seemed to be always fighting off an infection.

I took trip after trip to my doctor, and we tested for everything. Nothing came back. He was completely stumped as to the cause of my problems, so he started sending me to specialists.

We thought perhaps I had caught some tropical disease on my travels, so I went to an infectious disease specialist. No luck. We tried an ear, nose and throat guy. Nothing. Other specialists and nothing there.

Along the way I had an intuition. "Doctor, please X-ray me, because I think the hospital left the bullet inside me. I feel like my body is trying to expel a foreign matter."

"Save your money," he replied. "They are crazy at Jackson hospital, but not that crazy."

Finally I went to a gastroenterologist, who wanted me to do an entire upper and lower GI series. As I was getting ready, the nurse noticed my scar, and inquired about the cause. I told her about the surgery for the gunshot wound, and she went ahead with my testing.

About twenty minutes later, she came back in, holding up my X-ray. "I see they left the bullet inside you," she casually mentioned. "Is that because it's located right next to your spine?"

Imagine my shock, then anger. I had been sick for months and months. I had no insurance, and had spent everything I had on doctors, tests and specialists. I hadn't had a good night's sleep for so long I couldn't remember. And to think that the doctor had actually told me they took the bullet out! How could he lie to me like that?

I was very confused and not sure where to turn. I had malpractice lawyers lined up ten deep to take my case. It looked like a sure out-of-court settlement for a million dollars easy.

But this was after I had discovered "The Dynamic Laws of Prosperity" book. So like I always did when I needed guidance, I just closed my eyes. Flipped the pages and stuck my finger in to select a passage to read.

It was on forgiveness.

And she actually discussed situations like being in a lawsuit with someone. I saw my million dollars swirling down the drain. She said that if you were holding onto resentment or revenge, you couldn't be open to receiving all your allotment of prosperity.

Intuitively, I knew this to be true. I spent about 30 minutes meditating on the situation. I realized that the doctors and medical team had taken out my appendix, and left the bullet in for whatever reason. But they had also saved my life.

I had been shot in a robbery, and taken to the hospital after losing a great deal of blood, my pulse was dropping and my heart had almost stopped beating. If they didn't intervene, I would have died. I realized that they had done the best they could, with what they had to work with, and the consciousness they had.

I wrote out an affirmation of forgiveness 13 times, and put it in my Bible to pray on. I released the resentment, and viewed the doctors and medical people in the light of God. And an amazing thing happened . . .

That night, I got a complete night's sleep, without waking up in the middle, for the first time since I could remember. I soon had another operation to have the bullet removed. But my health started improving dramatically, the day I forgave.

This law is greatly tied to the vacuum law. If you are holding on to revenge, love can't walk in. If you are hanging on to resentment, you are hanging on to being a victim. And if you are holding on to being a victim, there's no space in your mind to be a victor.

You must release the negative feelings, as they only eat you up inside, and prevent you from you good. Now let me ask you a question?

Who do you think most people have the hardest time forgiving?

If you answered themselves, then you responded as 99 percent or more of my seminar attendees do. And you are correct.

I don't know why so many people have so much difficulty forgiving themselves, but they do. And I did too.

But I came to understand that no matter how bad I thought I was, I had a Creator who had already forgiven me. And I knew that I must forgive myself and move on, or I would continue to manifest a life of misery, limitation and lack.

When someone comes to me, and his or her prosperity seems blocked, this is where I look first. Once they forgive themselves, prosperity opens up to them.

So three steps I can recommend you take right now.

1) Mentally forgive everyone you are out of harmony with.
2) Mentally ask for forgiveness from the people you have wronged in the past, gossiped about, or are involved in lawsuits or other disharmony with.
3) If you have accused yourself of failure or mistakes—forgive yourself.

Once these three steps are completed, the rich avenue of Divine prosperity will open wide for you!

Forgiveness Affirmations:

For others:

Forgiving love sets us free.

Divine love produces perfect harmony between us.

I behold you with eyes of love, and I celebrate your prosperity, and honor your innate Divinity.

For yourself:

God is only good, and wants only good for me.

I am forgiven by God's love unconditionally, and all is well.

I have grown in my consciousness, and release the old me. I forgive myself, and move forward to accept my abundance.

Chapter Nine
What Will You Let God Give You?

"Poverty is a sin."

Charles Fillmore shocked the religious community when he made that statement decades ago. And people are still shocked when I affirm it today. Yet if you translate the original Aramaic text of the Bible, you will learn that sin means to "miss the mark." The Course in Miracle describes sin as a lack of love.

I agree with both of those definitions, because I believe when you are poor, you are missing the mark, and rejecting the love your creator has for you. There is nothing spiritual about poverty. Poverty causes people to lie, cheat, steal, and even kill.

Success and prosperity are your true natural state. The person who is not successful is at odds with the Universe.

It is spiritual for you to seek prosperity. This desire is God tapping on your door, inviting you to come in. For in order for you to *receive* more, you must *become* more. In this desire for prosperity, you move forward on your path of spiritual awareness.

Man has never had a desire that somewhere in the providence of God cannot be filled. If this weren't the case, the Universe would break at its most vital point. God is not a punishing God that requires you to prostrate yourself and grovel before him. (No matter what some preachers may have told you.) The translation of "gospel" means good news. And that is what this book is about.

The good news is you have a Creator that wants you to be healthy, happy and prosperous. He has blessed you with everything you need to manifest all this on the physical plane.

You cannot be "treated" for prosperity. You must be open to receiving it.

As I look around my church, my city, my country and my world, I see a lot of people who are experiencing lack and limitation in their lives. I know that some of them look at me with jealousy, and wonder why I have been blessed with what they have not.

So why is that? Let's analyze that . . .

Is it because I work harder?

Not a chance. My mechanic, my massage therapist, and my maid work a whole lot harder than I do.

Is it because I have more education?

I doubt that very seriously. I have an eighth grade education and was expelled from high school. I know many people with multiple college degrees who are mired in lack and limitation.

Is it because I am a better person? Maybe God likes me better?

What do you think? Do you really believe that there is a God up there, or a Universal Jedi Council somewhere saying, "Ok Randy is a good guy, let's give him a Lamborghini, Mary hasn't been so good, so give her a Toyota. Give Randy some extra energy because he has playoffs today. As for that guy Mike, let's give him a really bad tumor!"

Of course the idea is ludicrous. We know that God and the Universe are good. No one is singled out for punishment. Everyone has the opportunity to manifest prosperity. So that brings us to the last possibility . . .

Is it because I am more spiritual?

Yes. But only in the sense that we receive abundance in proportion to how we understand and comply with the laws of prosperity, the laws of our being.

Everything is possible for you, not because you make a prayer, and God responds favorably to your plea. But because your faith in prosperous outcomes, is the key that unlocks the power to manifest, in you. Everything has its origins in mind.

Ideas are centers of consciousness. Your health, happiness, relationships, intelligence, financial situation and intelligence will all be determined by the thoughts you give precedence to, the ideas you birth in your mind.

Build on your awareness of spiritual laws and expand your faith in your own innate good, and the talents you are blessed with.   The "stuff" and things will come. And they will come in great abundance. But know that they come not at your <u>expense</u>, but at your <u>expanse</u>.   Your faith in right outcomes is the only belief you need.

I believe that faith is a superhuman power we possess—<u>a mind power with the ability to shape substance</u>. The foundation for every work is an idea. Faith makes the idea real to you and your subconscious mind. It even makes it real to others. Then when others have faith in the thing you are doing, selling or creating, they see it as worthy of their support. *This creates the power of the Mastermind, and greatly expands your prosperity power.*

God or the Universe does not grant your requests. They have provided for your prosperity already. There are no "miracles" as most people perceive them. Hoping for miracles is believing that you may benefit from some whimsical, capricious fluke from the Universe. Instead, *expect* the Universe to provide all you need in its own due and natural course, as you call upon that force.

Your prosperity is not tied to the economy, your job, your education, your boss, or your past. It is here now, for you to manifest as you choose to. You were born to be rich.

All things are possible because you have faith in them. This faith unleashes the prosperity forces in your own mind to live the laws that transcend human limitation and potential. It is not a question of how much God will give you. The real question is:

What will you let God give you?

-RG

About Randy Gage

For more than 15 years, Randy Gage has been helping people transform self-limiting beliefs into self-fulfilling breakthroughs to achieve their dreams. Randy's story of rising from a jail cell as a teen, to a self-made millionaire, has inspired millions around the world.

This compelling journey of triumph over fear, self-doubt, and addiction, uniquely qualifies him as an undisputed expert in the arena of peak performance and extraordinary human achievement. His story and the way he shares it, demonstrate the true power of the mind over outside circumstances.

Randy Gage is a modern day explorer in the field of body-mind development and personal growth. He is the author of many best-selling albums including, *Dynamic Development* and *Prosperity* and is the director of www.BreakthroughU.com.

People from around the world interact and receive personal coaching from Randy through "Breakthrough U," his online coaching and success program. As Dean of BreakthroughU.com, Randy provides insight into how to overcome fear, doubt and self-sabotage to reach success and achieve the highest level of human potential.

For more resources and to subscribe to Randy's free ezine newsletters, visit www.RandyGage.com

101 Keys to Your Prosperity

"Insights on health, happiness and abundance in your life."

You are meant to be healthy, happy and prosperous. Once you recognize and accept this, it is simply a case of learning the principles that abundance is based on.

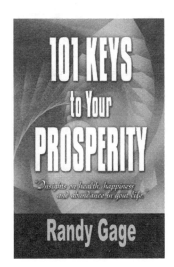

In this insightful book, Randy Gage reveals 101 keys to manifesting that prosperity in your own life. You will move from lack consciousness to living in the light of true abundance. You'll discover:

- What creates prosperity consciousness;
- The universal laws that govern prosperity;
- Why you should embrace critical thinking;
- The secret to creating a vacuum for good; and,
- What it takes to manifest prosperity on the physical plane.

Order the print book or downloadable eBook online at www.Prosperity-Insights.com

Quantity pricing for paperback book:

1–9 books	$7.00 each
10–99 books	$6.00 each
100–499 books	$5.00 each
500–999 books	$4.00 each
1,000 + books	$3.00 each

Accept Your Abundance!
Why You are Supposed to Be Wealthy

"Claim the Prosperity That is Your Birthright."

Do you believe that it is somehow spiritual to be poor? One reading of this fascinating book will dissuade you of that belief fast. You'll understand that you are meant to be healthy, happy and wealthy.

Prosperity guru Randy Gage cuts through the religious dogmas to reveal why becoming rich is your spiritual destiny. You'll discover:

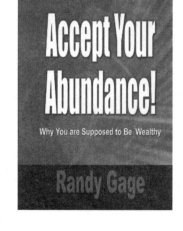

- Why poverty is a sin;
- What may be keeping you from your prosperity;
- Why being wealthy is your natural state;
- The difference between the way rich and poor people think; and,
- How to attract and accept your true abundance!

**Order the print book or downloadable eBook online at
www.Prosperity-Insights.com**

Quantity pricing for paperback book:

1–9 books	$7.00 each
10–99 books	$6.00 each
100–499 books	$5.00 each
500–999 books	$4.00 each
1,000 + books	$3.00 each

Order Online at **www.Prosperity-Insights.com**
or call 1-800-432-4243 or (316) 942-1111

37 Secrets About Prosperity

"A revealing look at how you manifest wealth."

In this landmark book, prosperity guru Randy Gage unveils 37 little-known insights into the science of prosperity. Gage breaks it down into simple, understandable explanations, so you can apply the information in your life immediately to create your own prosperity. He reveals how he went from a dishwasher in a pancake house to a self-made multi-millionaire.

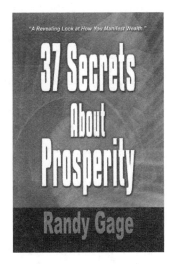

You'll learn:

- Why most people remain poor;
- How the rich leverage their prosperity;
- Why you should emulate certain business models;
- What separates broke, sick and unhappy people from the rich, healthy and happy ones; and,
- How you can manifest prosperity in all areas of your life.

Order the print book or downloadable eBook online at www.Prosperity-Insights.com

Quantity pricing for paperback book:

1–9 books	$7.00 each
10–99 books	$6.00 each
100–499 books	$5.00 each
500–999 books	$4.00 each
1,000 + books	$3.00 each

Prosperity Mind!

How to Harness the Power of Thought

"Brilliant Insights on health, happiness and abundance in your life."

Since "Think and Grow Rich" people have been fascinated with the power of the mind to accomplish great things. Now a recognized expert in human potential cracks the code on how you program yourself for prosperity!

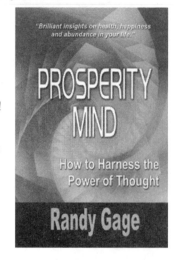

In this breakthrough book, prosperity guru Randy Gage reveals how you can actually program your subconscious mind to move from lack consciousness to prosperity thought. In it, you'll discover:

- How to identify self-limiting beliefs that hold you back;
- The 5 common expressions you probably use every day, which program you for failure on a subconscious level;
- How to practice the "vacuum law" of prosperity to attract good in your life;
- Imaging techniques to manifest things you want; and,
- How you can actually program your own subconscious mind for riches!

Order the print book or downloadable eBook online at www.Prosperity-Insights.com

Quantity Pricing for paperback book:

1–9 books	$7.00 each
10–99 books	$6.00 each
100–499 books	$5.00 each
500–999 books	$4.00 each
1,000 + books	$3.00 each

The 7 Spiritual Laws of Prosperity

"Live your life by the universal laws that govern health, happiness and abundance."

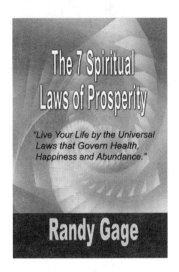

It is your birthright to be healthy, happy and prosperous. Accept this truth and it's simply a case of learning and living by the 7 Spiritual Laws that govern abundance.

In this breakthrough and insightful book, Randy Gage reveals the secrets behind harnessing these laws to manifest your own prosperity. You'll learn about each of these Prosperity Laws and discover how to:

- Create a vacuum for good;
- Use imaging to get what you want;
- Find and keep your perfect soul mate;
- Use creativity to get the bills paid; and,
- Attract money, health and harmony to your life.

Order the print book or downloadable eBook online at www.Prosperity-Insights.com

Quantity Pricing for paperback book:

1–9 books	$7.00 each
10–99 books	$6.00 each
100–499 books	$5.00 each
500–999 books	$4.00 each
1,000 + books	$3.00 each

The Prosperity Series
by Randy Gage

You are meant to be healthy, happy and prosperous. Once you recognize and accept this, it is simply a case of learning the principles that abundance is based on.

In this insightful series, you will move from lack consciousness to living in the light of true abundance.

Randy Gage reveals . . .

- What creates prosperity consciousness;
- The universal laws that govern prosperity;
- Why you should embrace critical thinking;
- The secret to creating a vacuum for good;
- What it takes to manifest prosperity on the physical plane; and,
- Why you are supposed to be wealthy.

Get all five books now and start living a life of abundance!

Order The Prosperity Series by Randy Gage online:

www.Prosperity-Insights.com

The Prosperity Series, 5 print books $30
The Prosperity Series, 5 eBooks $20
The Prosperity Series, all 5 print books and eBooks
Combination Special $47

Prosperity:
How to Apply Spiritual Laws to Create Health, Wealth and Abundance in Your Life
by Randy Gage

This album will help you uncover the subconscious "lack" programming you have that is holding you back. Then, you'll replace it with prosperity consciousness to manifest money, health, great relationships, happiness, and strong spiritual harmony.

True prosperity comes from understanding and living by the spiritual laws that govern our world. This album takes you through each of the Seven Spiritual Laws that govern prosperity—and shows you how to apply them. You will discover the ancient secrets to manifest prosperity in your own life.

You'll discover:

- Why you're supposed to be rich;
- The secrets of optimum health;
- How to get out of debt;
- The Seven Spiritual Laws you must live by;
- Your special powers for prosperity; and,
- How to image—then manifest—boundless, limitless prosperity.

This album will take you on a journey of spiritual enlightenment. You'll learn the practical applications so you can manifest prosperity in your life NOW! You'll learn about faith, the principle of attraction, and even how to use creativity to get the bills paid! This is the most specific, detailed and comprehensive album ever produced on how to become prosperous. **Don't you need it now?**

Prosperity: 8 CDs #A28CD $107
Prosperity: 8 audio-tape album #A28 $97

Order Online at **www.RandyGage.com**
or call 1-800-432-4243 or (316) 942-1111

Dynamic Development
Achieve Your True Potential with the Dynamic Development Series
by Randy Gage

Do you live a life of joy—or simply get through the week? Can you communicate well with your family and co-workers, or do you struggle to be heard? Are you in open, honest and loving relationships, or do you hide behind a mask? <u>How much more can you earn, learn, love and accomplish</u>? *If you want to break out of self-imposed limitations and break through to your true potential—the **Dynamic Development Series** is the perfect resource for you.*

Instantly hailed when it was released as the ultimate self-development resource, this is a two-year program to nurture your personal growth and achieve your innate greatness. Each month you will receive an audiotape from human achievement expert Randy Gage with a lesson, and some "homework" to complete that month.

It's a continuing journey on your path of personal development. Each month will bring you on an in-depth study in some area of human achievement, whether body, mind or soul. You'll discover new truths about yourself and uncover old ones. You'll desire more, obtain more, and accomplish more . . . by becoming more.

Dynamic Development, Volume 1, 12 audio-tapes
#V2 $147

Dynamic Development, Volume2, 12 audio-tapes
V4 $147

BEST DEAL! Both Dynamic Development Volumes, 24 audio-tapes #V2V4S $247

Crafting Your Vision

Twelve success experts share their secrets to success . . .

As soon as this 12 audio-tape album was released, it was hailed as one of the greatest self-development tools since *Think and Grow Rich!* It gets to the real root cause of success or failure—the vision you create for yourself.

It's pleasing to your ego to assume your prosperity is not growing because of outside factors and other circumstances. **But the truth is—you are reaping the results of the vision you created!**

Your suffering, frustration or failure to reach goals is the result of a neutral or negative vision—just as the blessings in your life are the results of a positive vision. This is an immutable, unshakable universal law. Living the lifestyle of your dreams begins with crafting the vision of where you want to go. For without a clear, compelling vision you simply cannot achieve what you're truly capable of. And there simply is no better resource to help you create an empowering vision for yourself than this amazing resource.

You'll learn how to craft your personal vision, how to design a vision big enough to encompass the visions of your people, and the steps to take on a daily basis to bring your vision to reality. You'll hear 12 complete programs on vision—recorded live—from 12 of the foremost experts on direct selling, recruiting and marketing.

This breakthrough album includes talks by:

Richard Brooke	Michael S. Clouse	Rita Davenport
John Milton Fogg	Matthew Freese	Randy Gage
Lisa Jimenez, M.Ed.	John Kalench	John David Mann
Jan Ruhe	Tom Schreiter	Tom Welch

 When you finish, you'll really know how to craft and manifest the vision of where you want to go. Make sure this resource is in your personal development library. **Get it today!**

Crafting Your Vision–12 audio-tape album #A30 $97

Get Randy Gage As

The only ongoing education program specifically designed for your success! Get personal, individualized success coaching from **Randy Gage**. Join Randy as he helps you expand your vision, shatter self-doubt, and reach your true success potential. Breakthrough U is your opportunity to have Randy as your personal success coach— mentoring you through the mindset, consciousness, and daily actions necessary to reach the success you are capable of.

Initiate Level

This is level one of an amazing journey of self-discovery. Each day you will receive a "Daily Awakening" e-mail message filled with mind-expanding exercises and success lessons to teach you how to think like ultra-successful people think. In addition to these "mind aerobics," you'll receive marketing tips, prosperity secrets and just general success information on how to make it to the top.

You will also have access to the members-only forum on the site so that you can network with other success-minded individuals, and get an invitation to attend Randy's BreakthroughU Success Events.

This is priced inexpensively and is for the beginning success seeker. If you've faced adversity, are deeply in debt, maxed out on your credit cards, or simply starting the journey—this is the program for you. Randy created this level so that those who are down and out— but committed to getting "up and in" —have a vehicle to do so. It's a program to change your consciousness, one day at a time.

Now, if you are further along the path, and serious about reaching higher levels of success—you're ready to advance to...

Alchemist Level

Alchemy, if you'll remember, is the medieval philosophy of transmutation; converting base metals to gold. This is the level for you if you're seeking a transmutation in your life; converting base thoughts and desires into the thinking and actions that produce rich and prosperous outcomes.

(continued on the next page)

Order Online at **www.RandyGage.com**
or call 1-800-432-4243 or (316) 942-1111

Your Personal Coach!

Like the Initiate Level, you will receive the Daily Awakening messages, access to the members-only forum, and an invitation to Randy's Success Convention. You will also receive:

- The "Alchemy Transmutation Kit" (with the intro lesson, CDs and binder);
- Subscription to the monthly lessons;
- Access to the monthly online video seminars;
- Monthly Tele-seminars
- Two Personalized Consultations

Now, if you're serious as a heart attack about success, and want to get even more individualized and personal coaching...you might want to consider the pinnacle level:

Mastermind Council

This is Randy's "inner circle" of select consulting clients, business partners, and colleagues. They receive a package of benefits so lucrative, that it's never been offered anywhere before. Membership in the **Mastermind Council** gives you a chance to get the most personalized help and guidance from me individually— as well as interacting with some of the brightest entrepreneurial minds on the planet.

In addition to the same benefits as the Alchemist, you will also receive:

- Ten Personalized Consultations;
- The chance to participate in twelve live Mastermind Conference Calls a year;
- Members-only Council Updates; and,
- The chance to participate in the Mastermind Retreats each year.

For complete details go to:
www.BreakthroughU.com

Randy Gage's
B BREAKTHROUGH U™

The Midas Mentality:
Expecting and Accepting Your Abundance

This program is the first resource of its kind, ever developed in the world. It will transform you from lack and limitation programming to prosperity consciousness. For 31 days, Randy Gage will work with you, helping you g through the same transformation that he did. He will help you peel away limiting beliefs and replace them with beliefs that serve you and he will help you identify fears and conquer them.

And level upon level, he will guide you in a metamorphosis of your thought process—from how sick, unhappy and broke people think—to the way healthy, happy, rich people do.

30 Audio CDs, 2 DVDs, Study Guide & Randy Jr. CDRo

It is a multi-media format, scientifically developed to literally change the way you think. You will create new neural pathways in your brain, develop your critical thinking skills, and foster whole brain synchronicity between the two hemispheres of your brain.

You will develop the multi-millionaire's mindset, which is the first—and most critical—step to becoming open.

On day one, you'll watch the DVD entitled, "The Science of Manifesting Prosperity." Then you'll load the CD-ROM into your computer. This will cause the "Randy Jr" character to pop up on your computer screen once each day, giving you one of his 101 keys to prosperity.

Then on the next day, you'll start the first of 30 daily lessons on audio CD. You listen to each lesson, then go to your workbook and complete the day's task. On average, this will take you from 45 minutes an hour per day Do only one lesson each day, to ensure that it "sets," and you are at a different consciousness when you start the next day's lesson.

Following the thirty CDs and workbook lessons, you then watch the final DVD, "Putting Your Prosperity in Place." Of course the "Randy Jr." character will keep popping up everyday, to keep your thoughts on track.

Trust me when I tell you that you will be thinking entirely different than when you started. You will have the mindset of a multi-millionaire, the single most important step to becoming one. You see, you can't be treated for prosperity; you can only be open to receiving it. By the time you finish this program, you will be. Really.

The Midas Mentality—30 audio CDs, 2 DVDs, Study Guide & Randy Jr. CDRom $997

Order Online at **www.ProsperityUniverse.com**
or call 1-800-432-4243 or (316) 942-1111

Randy Gage's Recommended Resources	Price	Qty	Total
Prosperity by Randy Gage **Select:** ¨ **audiotapes or** ¨ **CD's**	$97 (tapes) $107 (CDs)		
The Midas Mentality 30 day prosperity program	$997		
Dynamic Development Series Volume One by Randy Gage	$147		
Crafting Your Vision 12 audiotape album	$97		
Prosperity Series 5 books	$30		
101 Keys to Your Prosperity book	$7		
The 7 Spiritual Laws of Prosperity book	$7		
Prosperity Mind! book	$7		
Accept Your Abundance! book	$7		
37 Secrets About Prosperity book	$7		

United Parcel Shipping Table			

United Parcel Shipping Table

Order Total	2-Day	Ground
$50.00 or under	$11.60	$5.50
$50.01-$250.00	$13.20	$6.00
$250.01-over	$16.20	$7.00

Subtotal

$_____

For Alaska, Hawaii, and Canada - regular shipping cost, and add 10%. For foreign and overseas orders, figure the total of your order, plus the regular shipping cost, and add 20%

Shipping
(see chart)

$_____

Terms: 60-day money back guarantee! Contact us within 60 days of your invoice date if, for any reason, you're not 100% satisfied with any product you've received from us. Product must be in re-sellable condition. Customer Service: 1-800-946-7804 or (316) 942-1111

$_____
TOTAL

PAYMENT TYPE: ¨ **Visa** ¨ **MC** ¨ **AMEX** ¨ **Discover** or ¨ **Cash** ¨ **Check**

Please print clearly
Credit Card # __ __ __ __ __ __ __ __ __ __ __ __ __ __ __ __

Expires: (MM/YY) ____/____ Signature:_____

Full Name:

Address: Apt./Suite#

City: State: Zip: Country:

Phone: Email:

Ordering & Customer Service: Prime Concepts Group Inc.
1807 S. Eisenhower St. • Wichita, Kansas 67209-2810 USA
1-800-432-4243 or (316) 942-1111 • Fax: (316) 942-5313
www.ProsperityUniverse.com